AF491467

MY BEAUTIFUL CHAOTIC MIND

KYRSTEN McGEE

MILTON & HUGO L.L.C.
1001 3rd Avenue West, Suite 430
Bradenton, FL 34205, USA

Website: *www. miltonandhugo.com*
Hotline: *1- 888-778-0033*
Email: *info@miltonandhugo.com*

Ordering Information:
Quantity sales. Special discounts are granted to corporations, associations, and other organizations. For more information on these discounts, please reach out to the publisher using the contact information provided above.

Library of Congress Control Number: 2025915239
ISBN-13:   979-8-89285-598-3   [Paperback Edition]
                979-8-89285-596-9   [Digital Edition]

Rev. date: 03/18/2026

DEDICATIONS

I am dedicating these pieces of literature to every individual who may overthink, have self-esteem issues, have a difficult time expressing themself, be in a rough patch in life, have some unhealed trauma, or if you simply enjoy very raw material; this is for you. You are not alone. There are others similar to yourself. Your hardships will not last forever. One can find many different ways to cope with and heal whatever you're going through. Let your struggles fuel your creativity. Allow your overthinking to become art. Flourish in your pain and let it become your strength. It is okay to not be okay. It is okay to simply exist and take up space within this world. It is okay to not know what to do next. Close your eyes, take a deep breath and flip through these pages. Something you stumble upon might just help.

CONTENTS

INTRODUCTION

**"Whatever words come to mind,
may they flourish through these
pages and until the end of time."**

The following pages shall be filled with the anxiety and chaos that is also beauty and art from the deepest depths of my mind. It will be raw and vulnerable. My writing is a reflection of my growth and healing; it is a reflection of my journey. It is also a way to express the way I feel without exactly saying what I feel all of the time. These however are not exactly poems; they are more so quotes, sayings, or times I simply needed to write out my emotions with a sprinkle of poetry. If at any point in time someone decides to read this, I hope you enjoy my craziness.

SECTION ONE

THE STORM WITHIN

The wind doesn't warn before it shakes you. These pages hold the turbulence of the mind—loneliness, confusion, and the fragile search for identity.

A FADED SMILE

I used to be a carefree person; I never worried about much. I always smiled, I had such a pure heart. Now I'm this antisocial person who rarely speaks or smiles. I still have that big pure heart, but it's been broken and shut down for years. I'd like so much to be the same girl I was years ago when I smiled so much.

INNER REFLECTION

One day you're beautiful, and the next day you're an old hag. Trust me that is only how you feel, you are truly beautiful as everyone else on this earth. We are all beautiful in our own way, we are all equal and important. Everyone matters.

MY WAY

I drown myself in pain and sorrows. I do it alone in fear of being a burden to others. My mental health declines, my humor rises and I'm then seen as a ray of sunshine. I cry alone in the dark and come to the light smiling so no one can see my pain, so I don't have to explain why I stay in bed all day and eat my life away. I drown myself in sorrows and in pain, doing it this way... my way, it keeps me sane.

POV

Some say I'm annoying, and some say I'm shy. The truth is I'm both; if I don't know you I won't talk to you because I'm not very comfortable in new surroundings. Once I get to know you though, you won't be able to get me to shut up. I'm a pretty chill, timid person but if you want to get to know me this is a warning... be careful!

DARK, DIM, BRIGHT

Yesterday was dark, today is dim, but tomorrow will be bright. You have yet to see the light. Deep down inside is someone who is happy and free, someone you wish you could be. You should let that side of you out more often, maybe then your heart will soften. There's no need for another long, sleepless night because yesterday was dark, today is dim, but tomorrow will be bright.

A LITTLE ON EDGE

If someone tries to drag you down, drown them. Drown them in their sadness and the fact that they have no life.

THE REALIZATION

Sometimes you feel as if your world is crashing down and you're on the verge of breaking until you realize who you are and what you're capable of. You realize that you are stronger and more powerful than you know, and you can in fact rise above all.

MIRROR FIRST

Who said you had to judge people by their skin tone or what they wear? If you're going to judge people, start with yourself. You shouldn't judge others before figuring yourself out first.

THE BELIEVER

People think I'm crazy, they call me a fool because I believe in things others thought could never be true. I believe in love and second chances, but you will not take my kindness for granted. I choose optimism, negativity is a waste of time. If you want to reach your goals there will always be a climb. Love at first sight is such a cliché, but people like me believe in it anyway. People think I'm crazy, they call me a fool. People who don't understand me just aren't as cool.

A LONG LOOK IN THE MIRROR

I hurt people I cared about. I hurt the person I love. I hurt myself in the midst of trying to love myself. I can never be forgiven for any of it, because some scars never heal.

MY BEAUTIFUL, CHAOTIC MIND

I have so much to say yet my words escape me. My feelings overwhelm my body, and I feel so vulnerable yet protected. I am caged up, yet I am free. I hide my feelings from the world, yet I share so much about me. My brain is clogged with thoughts, yet so perfectly clear. I am blinded by the world's beauty, yet I see all of its tragedies. I am so cheerful and confident, yet sorrowful and confused. The world around me is changing and there's nothing I can do. I speak my mind, yet I silently observe everyone else. I am the center of attention, yet I blend in with the crowd. I used to chase people, but that's how I lost my crown. I have so much to say yet my words escape me. My feelings on display, for everyone to see. My emotions splattered all over these pages- but then I realized... that's just me.

SECTION TWO

LONGING, LOVE & LOSS

When the heart wants what it cannot have, the ache becomes art. These pieces are letters to lovers, ghosts, and the quiet ache of being unseen.

OH HOW BADLY

Oh how badly I want to be called beautiful by others who don't share the same blood as I, others who aren't close family friends. Oh how badly I want to be important to someone who is important to me. Oh how badly I want someone to call my own, someone I've dreamt of all of my life. Oh how badly I want to be in love.

WHY

Out of everything that could go through one's mind, why do you have to be running through mine? All you do is frustrate and confuse me, so why do I still think of you? Why do I care about what you think of my outfit? Why do I want you to notice my hair? Why do I care if you're here or if you're there? It seems I'll never know, but I am certain you're my 4th confusing disappointment in a row.

FATAL ATTRACTION

Everytime I see you, I just want to see you more. Although I know you're bad for me I want to be near you so badly. Your presence is enough to make me blush and get nervous. Hearing you speak sends shivers down my spine. Your confidence is incredibly attractive and your smile drives me crazy. Although I know you're bad for me, I can't help but to think of you.

100 THOUGHTS

100 thoughts going through my head and you are 99 of them. The thought of you liking me is so incredibly hard to believe. I think of you all of the time, you're the only thing on my mind. Everytime I see your face, my heart and pulse begin to race.

HOLDING ONTO HOPE

My friends say I should lose the thought of you, and although I know I should let you go, a part of me still has hope. When I look into your eyes I see comfort and compassion that no one else can see, and it'll be hard to find that in someone else when the only someone I care about is you. I still believe we have a chance so I'll be here until the very end, and even then I'll still care about you because that's just who I am.

LOVE COMES SLOWLY

How can people find love so easily? I've been trying to find someone I can call my own for some time now. All I've gotten in return is heartbreak and betrayal over and over again. I want someone to love, someone I can hold, and kiss, and hug. Someone who makes me smile and laugh, someone who never wants to make me feel bad. Someone who loves me in every way, someone who thinks of me and only me everyday. How can people find love so easily? For me, it feels like an eternity.

WHY DO I DO THIS TO MYSELF

Loving you has caused me so much pain, I'm starting to think I like to feel hurt. Our relationship has caused so much confusion, I'm starting to think I like feeling dumb. I want to let you go, but I want to stay and love you much more. I want to show you what real love is and heal all of your hidden scars. I don't want to keep being taken for granted and hurt, but I want you to learn to love someone properly. I want that someone to be me.

ISN'T THAT SAD

I think about you all of the time, even when I tell myself not to. I can't help but love you, even when I know I shouldn't. I can't help but dream about you and hope you'll do better so we can be together again. You're all I want, but I know I shouldn't have. I keep thinking maybe I should move on, but I don't want to. I want you and only you. Isn't that sad?

UNFORTUNATE

I still love you, but I'm afraid to say it out loud. If I say it I'll just confuse you more. I'm mostly afraid of you not loving me back. I miss you dearly, but I keep it to myself so no one can judge me. I wonder if you still love me like I love you, because I do... still really do love you.

CONFLICTING THOUGHTS

My heart tells me to slowly let you back in, my head tells me to leave you be. My heart tells me to text you, my head tells me to wait until you text me. I want to trust you, give you another chance, yet so many people tell me not to give you another glance. I want to love you, but I don't want to get hurt. I can't tell if the break up or missing you is worse.

TRY AGAIN

Although our love is different, and some might say it's wrong, we've come so far and both can't help but hold on. Hold onto the memories and all of the good times. Hopefully we'll make it through these storms and to the end of time.

DO YOU CARE

Through all of the chaos and confusion you say you still care. Where was that care when I needed it to be there? You say you care, but how will I know? Especially if emotions are hard for you to show. I want to believe you, I really really do, but I can't do that without trusting that you care for me like I care for you.

HEARTBREAK FOR FUN

You don't know me, yet you act like you do. You try to control me, yet you don't know how to. People try to tell me what to do, just like you. I provide for myself and depend on no one, because in the end everyone only talked to me for fun.

TAKE IT ALL BACK

You've turned into someone I don't even know. I miss the person you used to be, the one who cared about me. Now it's like you're a stranger, like we never met. I wish I could take back all of my time and energy, and I do mean all of it.

THE END OF A CHAPTER

My heart has never truly processed what happened between me and you. I don't think it ever will. Trying to forget about someone you knew you would always love is the hardest thing I've ever had to do. No matter what I do, or think, or say- I still love you, and think about you, and miss you every day.

SECTION THREE

BREAKING POINTS

Pain doesn't always break you—it teaches you where to draw the line. This section shows how boundaries are born in the dark.

ACCESS DENIED

The people who put you down try to come back into your life when you're doing good because they think you're going to forgive them. The truth is you've probably already forgiven them, but you've also forgotten them.

STAND YOUR GROUND

People will try to bring you down, but if you stay strong and don't ever back down you will conquer anything.

CHOOSE WISELY

People who make you cry are the people who want to ruin your life. The people who make you laugh just want you to feel loved and cared for. Which one do you want in your life?

SECRET ADMIRERS

Always remember that the people that hate you the most are secretly your biggest fans. They like you so much that it sickens them, and that's where the "hatred" comes from. They don't want you to succeed, but you do it anyway and it sickens them even more. Always remember, your haters are your biggest motivation.

A SMALL HIT

Just when you think love conquers all it shoots you down and burns you. It hurts but I live to love another day.

LOVE

People say love conquers all, but it tears people down and tears them apart. Love makes people do crazy, sometimes unforgivable things. Love can become an addiction and can get out of hand if not kept under control. People say love conquers all, although that may be true, love is a dangerous thing and can drive someone mad.

FULFILL THYN DESTINY

My love and compassion can only go so far. Determination and focus can take me the rest of the way to fulfill my destiny. Along with some hard work, that is; if you wish to fulfill your destiny, as I hope you do, then you must allow these things to create your path too.

SKIN DEEP

Depending on the person, beauty can only go so far. You might be very beautiful, and people like you, but if your personality is ugly you won't get that far. It truly is very rare to find someone who is very beautiful and truly has a kind and pure heart. While others are pretty and seem to be kind when they really aren't kind at all.

A WOMAN'S TEARS

Rain is just a build up of women's tears from all around the world. Tears of sadness, tears of joy, tears of depression, and tears of endurance. Women take on so many roles in this time, sometimes they are both a mother and a father to their children, or they are the mothers in a corner crying because of the abusive relationship that she is trapped in. A woman's tears mostly means that she is fed up and can't go any further, so she starts over.

SECTION FOUR

HEALING & BECOMING

When the storm settles, the rebuilding begins. These pieces reflect healing, hard-earned self-awareness, and the courage to begin again.

STARTING OVER

I'm starting to finally heal, how great of a feeling it is. I don't cry as much at the thought of you. I talk to new people and feel no guilt. I'm starting to feel better.

IMPROVEMENT

Self-improvement is everything. Without it no one would be who they are. They improved themselves for good or will improve themselves in the future. Self-improvement is never ending, improve yourself until you are confident in who you are as a person. Improve yourself until you feel like you've improved enough for yourself, don't ever try to improve for someone else, because that's not improvement, that's approval.

BE YOUR OWN SUPPORT

Pick yourself up when you fall. Dust yourself off and keep going. Wake up on a positive note and try your best everyday.

ENCOURAGEMENT

If you stay focused and be determined, you can achieve anything. With the right guidance and skill you will be able to do things you've always wanted to do, and things you've never imagined you could do.

ENCOURAGEMENT 2

Be truthful with yourself and openly admit your faults. Learn from them and improve. Self-reflect and open up about your emotions, and feelings, and accept that it is okay to feel things and to not always be okay. Improve yourself, never try to prove yourself.

MORALS

Be open with your feelings, pure with your intentions, and let your loyalty run deep for those who matter most. Keep your head held high and always do your best. Be true to yourself.

NAYSAYERS

Everyone might say you can't make it, you won't be able to do much in life. You will soon see you can do anything you set your mind to. If you have enough determination you will go extremely far in life no matter what someone has told you. You prove them wrong and chase your dreams.

A LITTLE REMINDER

No matter what someone tells you, always know and believe in your heart, mind, and soul that you are strong, you are beautiful; you are worth more than money, more than gold. You are important in every way possible, and you don't let anyone tell you otherwise.

REALITY CHECK

You may seem close to your dreams, but if you aren't working hard enough your dreams will be further than before.

MY LEGACY

My light shall burn bright for all eternity. My knowledge shall fill others' brains with ideas and creativity. My love shall touch other people's hearts and spread throughout the world, giving everyone that same special feeling.

AN EPIPHANY

This man is someone I never thought I'd meet. After all of my failed talking stages, seeking validation, a bitter-sweet relationship, and an on and off situationship I never imagined I'd find someone who truly wants to be with me and treat me well. I've gone through so much in life and I can finally say I see my life improving and becoming better. You truly attract who you are and what you allow, and I know that now. I hope this one lasts because it finally, actually, truthfully, sincerely feels right this time.

A SOFTER WORLD

Life would be so much easier if people listened instead of just reacting, if people spread love instead of hate, if people were careful instead of careless. Life would be better if people were more like you and me.

SECTION FIVE

WORDS TO HOLD ONTO

Not every truth needs to scream. Some whisper, quietly and clearly, what we need to hear. These final pieces are small anchors for big emotions.

POSITIVE AFFIRMATIONS

May your heart be strong, your head held high, your mind free, and your spirit wild. May your goals be reached so you can touch every star in the sky.

BUBBLES

Pain turns into determination, tears turn into fuel, bad vibes circle around you, but you look at them and pop them like bubbles. Fear turns into strength, and strength is power.

TO TRULY LOVE SOMEONE

To truly love someone is to understand and accept their flaws and faults. It's to understand that there will be boring days or bad days, and get through them. To truly love someone is to love them and choose them every day unconditionally and wholeheartedly.